MW01274165

Terry Tatum is a Stanford graduate, physician, and poet living in Middle America. As a youngster, he lost his father to the Vietnam War. This tragic event colored his life and the lives of his sisters and mother in many important ways. His own PTSD has inspired the themes of loss, wartime chaos, environmentalism, diversity, cultural reflection and criticism, childhood idealism, and restitution prevalent throughout his poetry. Terry hopes that others will be inspired by this book to reflect their own truth in kind and creative ways.

This book is dedicated to our parents, Lawrence Byron Tatum and Mary Lee Tatum. To the one who died way too early and to the other who saved us.

Terry Tatum

THE PICTURED GIRL AND OTHER SHORT POEMS

AUSTIN MACAULEY PUBLISHERS™

LONDON • CAMBRIDGE • NEW YORK • SHARJAH

Ordering Information
Quantity sales: Special discounts are available on quantity purchases by corporations, associations, and others. For details, contact the publisher at the address below.

Publisher's Cataloging-in-Publication data
Tatum, Terry
The Pictured Girl and Other Short Poems

ISBN 9781638294863 (Paperback)
ISBN 9781638294870 (Hardback)
ISBN 9781638294887 (ePub e-book)

Library of Congress Control Number: 2023900682

www.austinmacauley.com/us

First Published 2023
Austin Macauley Publishers LLC
40 Wall Street,33rd Floor, Suite 3302
New York, NY 10005 USA

mail-usa@austinmacauley.com
+1 (646) 5125767

Many thanks to my friends at the local poetry salon: English professors Frank and Peggy Steele, Jim Skaggs, John Guzlowski, Dory Hudspeth, and Elise Talmage Lieb. Their own experiences expressed through poetry, and their kind and helpful advice, have been a great inspiration to me. Most of the poems in this book were written during my association with them.

Table of Contents

Preface

The Pictured Girl is an introductory book of poetry, specifically concerning the significance and power of short poems. These are typically poems which capture their themes or sub-themes in a few short stanzas or, at most, in a page or two. As such, they are entirely different in their construction, purpose, and effect from other longer poems. One can say, for instance, that a short poem of the type selected for this book is as different from the slowly evolving and building drama of an epic poem as a photograph is from a three-hour motion picture. Both have their importance and impact but achieve them in different ways.

To use another visual analogy, a short poem is often constructed and consumed in a way similar to a newspaper or magazine cartoon. The stanzas are used almost as sparingly as the frames of such a cartoon. The short poem author, whose themes are not always serious, and the cartoonist, whose themes are not always funny, has a small space and time in which to capture the reader's attention. He or she must distill their chosen theme in a measured way. Yet, the effect can be lasting. Many of us long remember a joke, cartoon, famous saying, or short poem heard or read only once. The human brain has a special place for appreciating and storing such gems.

One can best learn these things by reading a collection of short poems, as presented herein.

Terry Tatum
July, 2022

The Pictured Girl

I blew the dust away
And held the weathered frame
At angle in the light
To see the portrait well

I felt a sudden jolt
She seemed to look at me
Her lips appeared to form
A Mona Lisa smile

With trembling of my hands
I gently touched her face
I gazed into her eyes
And traced her sacred hair

I'd seen this face before
These eyes, these lips, this smile
I'd seen them every night
In fitful dreams awhile

Alas, the pictured girl
Was swimming in my tears
She was a soulmate lost
About a hundred years

Lesson on the Passing

I felt the warmth
Leave her hand
While she stared
Silently at the ceiling

It was then I learned
That tears cannot express
What is in the heart
The true depths of sorrow

For tears only wet the sheets
And leave behind a bitter salt
Sobs echo off deaf walls
And only wake the living

The lesson learned that day
For mother, sister, daughter
Wife or friend is
Love them while they're here

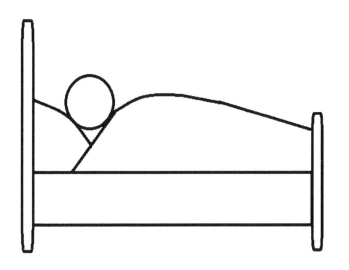

A Day at the Beach

Now that you're gone, all things are about you
I walk the seashore, your feet squish the sand
The seagulls above me all cackle with laughter
I toss them the bread I hold in your hand

I squint in harsh sunlight and pull out dark glasses
I balance them sure on the bridge of your nose
The fiddlers are dancing, they scurry right past me
They dodge and they weave when you wiggle your toes

I taste the salt spraying of waves that come crashing
In closing my eyes, I am kissing your lips
I smell in the breezes the sea so enchanting
But nothing so like your perfumed fingertips

Two lovers approaching are holding our hands
If only they knew what is rubbing me wrong
I pick up a seashell and listen intently
And all that I hear is your favorite song

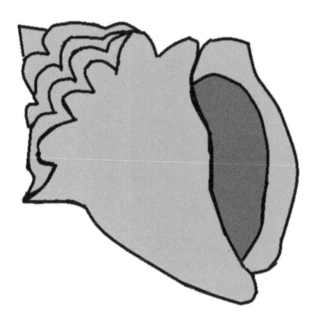

War Trilogy (In Stages)

1.   The Unremembered Visit (Denial)
My sisters weren't eating the orange sherbet
Nor I the lime
They were never our favorites
Nor were we watching *Bonanza*
On our new color TV

And Grandpa never yelled
"You kids go to the back bedroom"
When the priest and the uniformed officer
Who didn't get out of the Air Force staff car
Never pulled up to our house

And we never heard the knock
On the front door
Through the closed bedroom door
Nor the sobs of our mother
Nor the sound of her knees hitting the floor

2.   'Closure' (Anger)
Some slick shrink
Coined a term

Loved by the media
Hated by those who grieve
"Does this give you closure?"
They asked breathlessly
Shoving a microphone
In the faces
Of those left behind
In Oklahoma City
After McVeigh went to sleep

They could have asked the same
Of me when my father
Didn't come back from the war
And they handed my mother
A neatly folded flag and a medal
Except I stayed home
Even as a teenager
I knew that 'closure' wasn't hiding
In that piece of cloth
I will only find it
When they close the lid on me

3.   On the Wall (Acceptance)
In the town of monuments
I heard they built a wall
A place for fallen heroes
Who sacrificed their all
For those who had the courage
And never got their due
Who lived for God and Country
And died for me and you

Emboldened by the thought of them
I vanquished all my fears
And searched along the hallowed path
So humbled by the years
I knelt beside my father's name
And those of all his peers
I rubbed it with a piece of cloth
And blessed it with my tears

A Lesson in Chaos

Casting out determinism
We embrace complexity
And call it chaos

As chaos teaches
The low-hanging fruit
Of scientific law
Has already been picked
Are you listening
Mr. Newton?

The real world
Has chaos in the air
And we call it stormy weather
The real world
Has chaos in the water
And we call it rogue waves

The real world
Is really worlds within worlds
Holistic
Self-similar

And fractal

Chaos also teaches
The first casualty of war
Is the last nine steps
Of a ten-step battle plan
Is anybody listening?

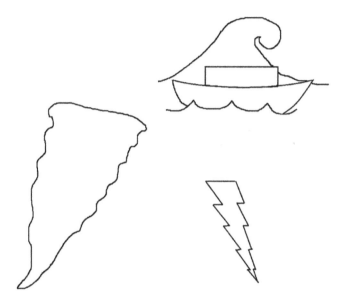

Recipe for War

1. First you start
   With a ripe misunderstanding
   Or a raw deliberate act
2. Add half-baked rumors
3. Sprinkle in some epithets
4. Then pour on the hostility
5. Stir gently
6. Let things simmer
   While the media
   Brings things to a boil
7. When the lid blows off
   It is ready to serve

A Note to J. Robert Oppenheimer

Did you really mean it, Bob
When, tears in your eyes,
You quoted the ancient scripture:
"Now I am become death,
Destroyer of Worlds"
Or was this feigned sympathy
After your great achievement
The physicist's dream
And the world's nightmare?

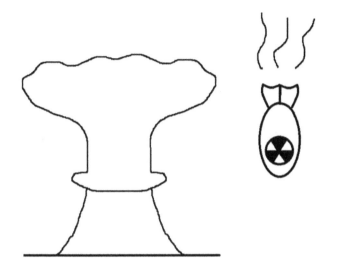

Just a Different Color

I stood on the hilltop
Field glasses in hand
Directed at the opposite ridge

How much the other line
Looked like our own
Just a different color

A second before my command
Just for an instant
They were my brothers

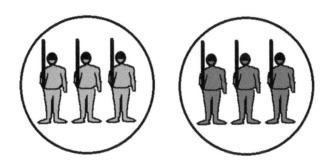

Copper Turned to Blue

Walking in the park
I came across a hero
Perched atop his metal horse
His copper turned to blue

And though I read his name
I knew not much about him
Save for those who loved him
It mattered not the hue

HERO

The World Is Blue

Beneath the azure sky
The melancholy world
Heaves a wistful sigh
To see a dream unfurled

Fed up with all man's ways
Of rampant greed and waste
She longs for virgin days
A time when She was chaste

For grasses and for trees
All tangled up in vines
For flowers full of bees
And scenery so sublime

But all that comes to view
Are asphalt fields obscene
Alas, the world is blue
But wishing She were green

Extinction

Extinction is the sound of change
Jingling into a cash drawer
The whispered 'checkmate'
Of an ivory king
It is the smell of exotic perfumes
And the taste of powdered rhino horn
An aphrodisiac for desperate men
In alligator boots

Extinction is also the sound of a chainsaw
Gnawing through a jungle
It is the sting of smoke in your eyes
When a brushfire burns a clearing
Or the bitter taste of acid in the rain
Finally, it is the rumble of heavy equipment
Felt first in your feet
And last in your heart

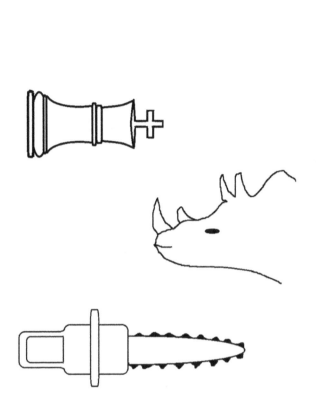

Burning Dinosaurs

Blood of ancient reptiles
Oozes from shale
And spurts from the tops
Of well-placed wells
Staining everything it touches

Shipped in barrels
It washes over our shores
Siphoned into the bellies
Of restless machines
Where it is burned
To a thin smoke curl
Which we never see
Head down
Pedal to the metal
To our own extinction

About the Trip

I find it best to travel
Without a map
But I am not without
My formula
Take a small red sports car
Tuned to 'Sultans of Swing'
Add a dash of cologne
Crank it up to speed
And set it on cruise control
Who needs a destination?

Mountain Retreat

I inhale the chilly air
Like a patient on life support
The smell of wet pine
Mixes well with hot coffee

Outside my cabin door
Mother robin hops the dew
Searching for worms I left behind
The worms I have will feed the fish
At the bottom of the holler

Before I walk the trail
With rod and reel in hand
I marvel how the hilltops
Look like islands in the clouds

Colorado Ghost Town

What dreams did your cabins hold
Long since gone
Through broken windows
Through gaps in unchinked logs
Like faith ripped from a believer?

How long did the cold wind curse
Your toil in the long-dead creek
At the bottom of the hill
While you panned
With stiff, cracked hands
Hope fading, head throbbing
In the high altitude, nothing
Even whiskey could cure?

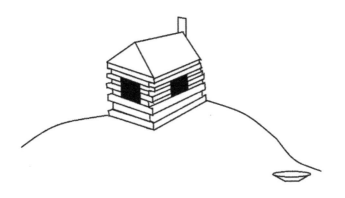

Cool as Diamonds

On hot summer nights
In my younger years
I opened my bedroom window
And leaned upon the sill

God's myriad stars
Were a source of wonder
Nearly within reach
They beckoned my wishes
And watched over me
Cool as diamonds

But now I know
About light-years
And hot hydrogen gases
And how God's choices
Have become Newton's laws
And that stars no longer care
About wishes and little boys

Offerings

In my infancy
My offerings were limited
But I brought you wonder
Introduced you
To Sid, Imogene, Ed, and Uncle Miltie
We had a few good laughs
At no one's expense
And don't forget Elvis
Maybe my noisy cousin
Had first dibs on his voice
But who brought you
Those crazy hips?

In my adolescence
I gave you growing pains
Bringing Camelot to an end
With a little boy's salute
And running soldiers
Through your living room
'Til even Cronkite had enough
But the wonder came back
With a small step

On the Sea of Tranquility

In my middle years
Almost drowned out by disco
I had little to show you
But an armchair bigot
And a sweater president
With a bad case of malaise
Except for Belushi and company
Raising hell on Saturday Nights

But now in my dotage
I've made a comeback
Amidst the dueling lawyers
The squabbling Senators
The raving lunatics
Of every persuasion
I offer you everything
Your heart desires
Twenty-four hours a day
Everything but the wonder

Master of the Air

Marconi claimed me
Though Tesla was
My true father
The custody battle
Outlasted both

I was a miracle
Before those Wright boys
Even flew
Mastered the air
While they were still tinkering
With bicycles

Speaking first in clipped tones
Set off by sparks
I shocked the world
When the great ship sank

Then I found my true voice
Sang tunes to farm families
And told everyone
About the Great War

Sure beat that Victrola
Caught even Mr. Edison
By surprise

The Radio Sport

Grandpa dropped everything
To tune in Ernie Harwell
On those warm Michigan nights

The dishes could wait
When the radio crackled
And our heroes were at work

Grandma didn't seem to mind
I saw her wink at me
When she turned to leave the porch
A tray of lemonade in her wake

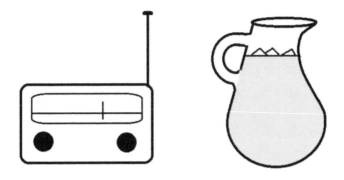

Airport Morning

I do not ponder
The wild blue yonder
Or charge the gate
To hear the engines whine

Nor do I chance
To see it dance
The sun off silver wings
Of magic metal birds

Instead, I turn my head
To steal a glance
This lonely dawn
To dwell upon
Two gentle souls
In last embrace

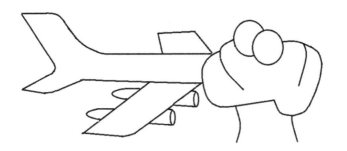

Philosophy

Before Newton
It was the love of all wisdom
After Newton
It was the love of all things
Impossible to measure
An awkward 'science'
Shrinking by the day
'Til eventually
Descartes decayed
Kant couldn't
And Spinoza spun away

Thunderstruck

Ernest and F. Scott
Didn't pay their dues
Not to say
That they weren't troubled
But that came mostly
Past their greatness
When others
Drunk on their celebrity
Tempted them

For those who believe
That writing is a craft
To be worked diligently
In the dead of night
Year by year
Draft by draft
These two seem
Especially cruel
God struck both
With greatness
In their twenties

So save your tickets
To the cafes of Paris
Discard your books
On Gertrude Stein
And the Lost Generation
Cancel your courses
In creative writing
Go outside
Grab a lightning rod
And pray

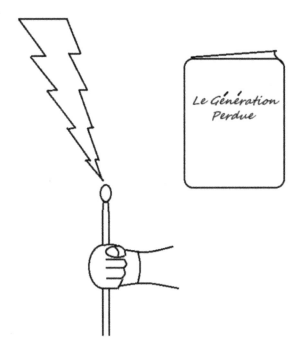

Le Génération
Perdue

Where Are the Cowboys?

Jesse the trucker
Gallops his Pony Express
Delivery van down I-80
Past Cheyenne and Laramie
Lookin' for smoky signals
On his radar detector
When the coast is clear
He lights one up
And yodels to Hank Williams

Shane the hustler
Blows the chalk off his cue
Like smoke from a gun
"Who's next?" he bellows
Through the haze
At the corner saloon
Stuffing another ten-spot
From a greenhorn
Next to his Marlboros

Wyatt the sheriff
Dismounts his Harley

On the highway shoulder
Behind the Mustang
He's just pulled over
Taking no chances
He clicks the safety on his gun
It's high noon and he's ready
For a showdown

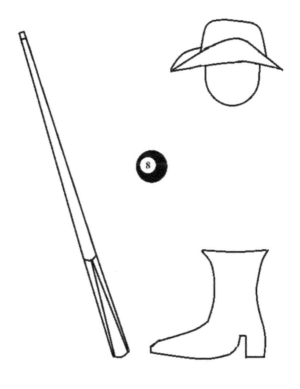

Questions for a
Ramshackle Barn

Ramshackle barn
What stories do you know
Born of sturdy hands
A hundred years ago?

Did you come into this world
By a raising dance and feast?
Were they bursting full of pride?
Did they toast you at the least?

As a child upon this hill
Did you watch the biplanes soar?
Did you hear the Model T
Come chugging by your door?

And in your junior years
Were there lovers in your loft?
Were they rolling in the hay
And cooing low and soft?

And in your middle age
Did your farm boys leave their chores?
Did they stop to say 'goodbye'
'Fore they left to fight the wars?

And when they came to rest
At the bottom of the hill
Did that make you feel bereft
And all the older still?

And now that you're unstable
And splitting at the seams
Can you tell me, if you're able,
If you realized all your dreams?

Punch Drunk

An uppercut has a way
Of loosening up your thoughts
Like the one that jolted him
For the last time

Before the mist
Of blood and sweat
Could clear the air
Even before his legs
Could turn to rubber
His mind went back
A hundred years ago
To that first day in the gym
When it was all laid out before him
Like a path to manhood

Chin leading the way
Halfway through the fall
He caught a fleeting glimpse
Of the glory he had dreamt
Of holding a shining belt
High above his head

High enough
For even Father to have seen

Outside the Wind Howls

Curled up cozy
Beside the fire
My book in hand
To most inspire

Outside the wind howls

With not a care
I turn the page
My cabin warm
Is all my stage

Outside the wind howls

For I am young
It matters not
That fires burn low
And logs can rot

Outside the wind howls

Freeze Frame

There are moments
Had I the powers
To halt the minutes
And freeze the hours
When I'd frame your face
Within my hands
And slow the pace
Of our life's dance

My magic wand
Against the sky
Would stop the sun
From going by
Becalm the wind
And water's wave
So that our time
Could all be saved

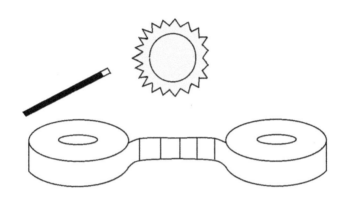

Photo Album

Time steals
What memory fails to hold
Until faces
Long pressed
Between hard covers
Smile their restitution

High Water Marks

moments
IN OUR LIVES
are much
LIKE THE TIDES
ebbing
AND FLOWING
toing
AND FROWING
marking
ON THE WALLS
of memory

My Creations

Like a parent
Filled with pride
These bright ideas
I held inside

Then came the time
To let them out
Into the world
Without a doubt

I wound them up
And set them down
Toy toddlers placed
Upon the ground

I could not say
Which way they'd go
And what results
I could not know

But I had faith
That butterfly wings

When given time
Whip up great things